The Happy Family, or, Winter Evenings' Employment

The Happy Family.

THE

HAPPY FAMILY;

OR,

Winter Evenings' Employment.

CONSISTING OF

READINGS AND CONVERSATIONS,

In Seven Parts.

BY A FRIEND OF YOUTH.

WITH CUTS BY BEWICK.

"O snatch your offspring from adding to the number of those objects
"of supreme commiseration, who seek their happiness in doing nothing."
HANNAH MORE.

YORK:

Printed by and for T. WILSON and R. SPENCE,
High-Ousegate. 1801.

(PRICE ONE SHILLING.)

PREFACE.

TO reprefent TIME as valuable; STUDY amufing and profitable; INTEGRITY indifpenfable; VIRTUE amiable; and the paths of RELIGION, as the ways of pleafantnefs; is the plan of this little work: and to draw the attention of young minds to thefe important views, is the motive for publifhing it. Should the work prove fuccefsful but in a fingle inftance, my labour will be rewarded.

I have enriched my little volume with paffages from a number of admired authors; particularly from the late incomparable work of Hannah More*. In felecting from this author, I rifk being claffed amongft the *"beauty mongers"* of the day; as, indeed, it is fcarcely poffible to felect a line

* Strictures on the Modern Syftem of Education, by Hannah More.

A 3

from that book, where the reader, if he has any difcernment, will not difcover a *beauty.* When I make extracts from this work, in order to illuftrate my fubject, particularly when that fubject happens to be religious education, it is becaufe no other author fupplies me with fentiments, which I deem fo well adapted to my purpofe. And I fhall fail exceedingly in my defign if the reader does not find in thefe paffages, fome things that may lead him to examine the work from which they are felected. There he will find not only beauty and elegance—but treafures of infinitely greater importance.

If I have borrowed a few tints from the moft fuccefsful Artifts that have ever painted the advantages of early reflection, I truft I fhall be forgiven. I have done fo in the hope that, by applying thofe bright touches, which cannot fail to attract, the whole of my little compofition may be recommended to the obfervation of thofe, for whofe amufement and edification it was defigned by

A FRIEND OF YOUTH.

WINTER TALES, &c.

THE FIRST EVENING.

ELDEST BOY.

NOW, my young friends, we are met together for our amusement, let us form some regular plan of proceeding. I am the oldest of the company, therefore I propose that we all sit round this cheerful fire, and read some entertaining stories out of the little book which has just been presented to us. This book, it appears, has been written by one who is a Friend of Youth: that being the case, we may expect to find something in it to entertain us; and, perhaps, while it makes us merry, it may also make us wise; and, what is more, may tend to make us good; and that, I have heard my father say an hundred times, will certainly make us happy.

We are here prefented with a fhort defcription of that noble animal the Lion : but before I begin to read, in order to engage your attention, you fhall fee the beautiful picture which is here placed at the top ; and as we perhaps may hear a great deal concerning this fierce looking animal, we fhall, by viewing his portrait, the better underftand what fort of a creature he is.

THE LION.

This animal is produced in Africa ; he reigns the fole mafter of the deferts his

rage is tremendous, his courage undaunt-
ed, and his roaring horrible. His mane is
large and fhaggy, and he is of a tawny colour; his ftrength is great: and yet for all
this ftrength and fiercenefs, becoming once
acquainted with man, and the power of
his arms, he lofes his natural fortitude, and
is terrified even at the found of the voice
of his keeper. Such is the fuperiority of
reafon over inftinct—fuch is the power
which Providence hath given to man over
the whole creation. However tame thefe
creatures appear, we ought not to truft
their favage nature too far. I will tell you
a little ftory about one of thefe animals.

STORY OF A LION.

A Gentleman once kept in his chamber
a Lion, which he fuppofed to be quite
tame; and his fervant, who ufed to feed
and attend it, as is ufual, mixed blows with
careffes. This ill-judged affociation continued for fome time. One morning, however, the gentleman was awakened by an
unufual noife in the room; and drawing
his curtains, he perceived it to proceed
from the Lion; which was growling over

the unhappy man, whom it had juft killed, and had feparated his head from his body.

This ftory the younger part of my readers fhould keep in mind; it may be the means of faving you a hand or an arm. You will perhaps frequently fee thofe fierce animals either at the Tower of London, or at Mr. Pidcock's, or carried about the country in iron cages: you will fee their keepers play with them and carefs them; and becaufe you obferve in the animal a fullen compofure, which you miftake for gentlenefs, you may approach too near the grate, and attempt to touch them; but be aware of doing fo; remember the Lion in the chamber; he may at that very time be watching an opportunity to feize you; and the lofs of an arm would be paying dearly indeed for your curiofity. Many accounts affure us that the anger of the Lion is noble, its courage magnanimous, and its temper fufceptible of grateful impreffions. This may be; but we have feen how little thefe noble qualities are to be depended upon: and when there is no good to be done, or glory to be gained, it is certainly fafe, prudent, and commendable to avoid danger; and at all times proper to keep at a diftance from bad company.

As the Lion is remarkable for his ftrength and fiercenefs, fo is the Moufe for its weaknefs and timidity. But to fhow you how the ftrong and hardy may be fometimes obliged to the weak and timid for their prefervation—and, indeed, how the high and mighty may occafionally be dependent upon the meek and lowly; or the rich and profperous faved by the charitable affiftance of the humble and grateful; I will here infert a little fable of—

A LION CAUGHT IN A NET.

A little, timid Moufe was amufing itfelf by picking up a few grains of rice, which had efcaped the hand of the gleaner, and were fcattered on the ground; without obferving a tremendous Lion who had fought this fhady place, and ftretched himfelf out to repofe. The little animal caught the Lion's attention. He gently laid his paw upon the moufe; which, in an agony of fear, in the moft pitiable language, implored his mercy, and begged him to fpare the life of an object fo inconfiderable as he muſt appear in the eyes of his majeſty.—"Go," ſays the Lion, "I did not intend to hurt thee; but keep this leſſon in thy mind, when any one is helping himſelf to that which is the property of another, there may be an eye upon him that he ſuſpects not." The Lion releaſed his little priſoner, who went away rejoicing at the clemency ſhown him by his royal maſter.

It happened a little while after this, that the Lion, who was prowling amidſt ſome thickets in the dead of night, fell into a ſnare, a net of ſtrong cords, which had been ſpread for the purpoſe. Finding himſelf thus enſnared, and unable to extricate himſelf, he ſoon made the woods reſound with the moſt horrible roaring. It was in vain he ſtrove to untie the knots which held him: the more he applied his ſtrength, the more firmly they were bound together.

His cries at length reached the ear of his little friend the Mouſe, whom he had ſo lately ſet at liberty. The voice was well remembered by the little animal; and without ſtopping to conſider in what way

fo infignificant a creature as he could ferve fo great a perfonage, or what rifk he would run of meeting his deftruction if he approached the Lion whilft thus enraged, he ran with all his fwiftnefs to the place; impelled by gratitude and a fenfe of duty, he difdained all fear. He foon faw in what condition the Lion was in.—
" Defpair not," fays he; " ceafe to fhake the earth with this terrible roaring: be ftill, and fuffer me to apply the means that occur to me for your deliverance." He immediately fell to work, and foon, with his fharp teeth, gnawed away the principal knots by which the Lion had been confined, fo that he could eafily fhake off the net. " Now," fays this little knight errant, " your majefty will pleafe to walk forth; and let this leffon teach you, that a charitable action done in fecret, feldom fails to be rewarded."

There is a pretty ftory told of a Lion, which, if true, ferves to fhow that he in his turn, is capable of gratitude. It is as follows:

There was a traveller who loft himfelf

in a foreſt: it was almoſt night; and having ſpied a cave, he went in to ſtay till
the next day: but a moment afterwards,
he ſaw a Lion coming towards the cave.
The man was in a great fright, and thought
that the Lion was going to devour him.
The Lion walked on three feet, and held
up the fourth; he came thus to the traveller, and ſhowed him his paw, in which
there was a large thorn; the man took
out the thorn, and having torn his pocket
handkerchief, wrapped the Lion's paw in
it. This animal, by way of thanking him,
fawned upon him like a dog, did him no
harm, and the next day the man went
his way. Some years after, the man, for
ſome crime he had committed, was con-
demned to be torn by wild beaſts. When
he was in a place called the Arena, they let
out againſt him a furious Lion, which at
firſt run at him to devour him: but when
he came near the man, he ſtopped to look
at him; and knowing him to be the ſame
who had taken the thorn out of his foot,
he went up to him, moving his head and
tail, to ſhow the pleaſure he had in ſeeing
him again. The emperor was very much

surprifed at this fight; and, having ordered the man to be brought to him, he afked him if he knew the Lion; the criminal gave him an account of the adventure, and the emperor pardoned him.

There is not a more pleafing exercife of the mind than gratitude. It is accompanied with fuch inward fatisfaction, that the duty is fufficiently rewarded by the performance. It is not like the practice of many other virtues, difficult and painful, but attended with fo much pleafure, that were there no pofitive command which enjoined it, nor any recompenfe laid up for it hereafter,—a generous mind would indulge in it for the natural gratification that accompanies it. If gratitude is due from man to man, how much more from man to his Maker ? The Supreme Being does not only confer upon us thofe bounties which proceed more immediately from his hand, but even thofe benefits, which are conveyed to us by others.— Every blefling we enjoy, by what means foever it may be derived, is the gift of Him who is the great Author of Good and Father of Mercies.

ELDEST BOY.

The Evening is now pretty far advanced, and I think we cannot leave off at a better place. I muft own the delight I feel in thofe charming reflections; they will for ever be imprefled on my mind, and I hope they will alfo be imprefled upon your minds. We fhould be ungrateful to the Author of this little book, which has already afforded us fo much entertainment, if we did not make a proper application of thofe virtuous fentiments.—How indeed can we clofe the evening better, than by exprefling our thanks to the Father of all Mercies, through whofe kind providence we have been rendered fo happy this night, and from whom we have received fo many, many blefings.

THE SECOND EVENING.

ELDEST BOY.

WELCOME, my little brothers, fiſters, friends!—with pleaſure I meet you again, to renew our Evening's Converſation, and proceed in our entertaining and inſtructive little book. Here it is—

" *Am I not a Friend and a Brother?*"

On opening the part which contains the ſecond evening's reading, I obſerve the picture of a Negro: poor fellow, he seems to be in great distress.—Hand him round before I begin to read concerning him.

ELIZA.—(6 YEARS OLD.)

O! what a disagreeable black looking creature! I never saw any thing so frightful; and all hung about with chains, I declare: I dare say he fancies himself my Lord Mayor, or some such fine man. I have no patience with such conceited things: and only see what faces he makes; most likely all this finery is very painful to him. It reminds me of our Margery, the cook, who was such a silly thing as to go the other day and have her ears bored; she came back making such faces as this. Mother told her that "pride was painful;" and I really think both Margery and this black man would look quite as well without having bits of brass wires hanging at their ears.

ELDEST BOY.

What you say of Margery may be very proper; but what you say of the poor

black man ferves to fhow how very cau-
tious we fhould be in forming our judg-
ment of perfons by their outward appearance, and of being too hafty to condemn.
This is the portrait of a poor negro flave,
who has been dragged from his country,
his connexions, and his friends. Perhaps
an affectionate hufband and a tender father, whofe haplefs family are bemoaning
his lot in fome remote corner of the world;
or who may, by this time, be loaded with
chains, and under the tyranny of fome cruel
tafk-mafter, obliged to lead a life of flavery
like his, in order that fuch as you may
have fugar to your tea, and your tarts made
fweet and palatable.   Now there is little
Harry, with his pink and white cheeks,
and his fparkling eyes, fuppofe fome great
rough looking man was to come and fteal
him away, and carry him into fome diftant
country, and when he was able to work,
load him with chains, as if he was a cart-
horfe. Would it not have coft you many
a forrowful thought, many a deep figh,
when you reflected that your brother was
torn from you, and fo cruelly treated? we
will fuppofe him carried away into a far

diftant clime, where fome little girl may
fay, "O! what a difagreeable *red and
white* looking creature!—how frightful!"
—This poor black man is the work of
the fame Creator as you are. There is,
to be fure, a very great difference in the
colour of your fkins; but as neither were
of your own making, fo neither of you
have any bufinefs to be proud of the difference, nor to defpife each other on account of it. He is a poor miferable creature, and deferves all our compaffion;
and fo do all his wretched race.

EDWARD—(EIGHT YEARS OLD.)

You have faid fo much about this poor
Negro, it makes me love him better than
if he was white. I could look on his picture, and reflect on his forlorn condition,
until I fhed tears over it.

ELIZA.

I'm fo forry to think that I fhould be fo
naughty as to call him names, I could cry
too. I wifh I could take thefe ugly chains,
and tear them link from link; and could
raife him up from his knees, I would kifs

him, and tell him, that though I was fo
filly to call him names, *I did not mean to
hurt him.* And when he faw my tears, I
think he would believe me.

ELDEST BOY.

It was fpoken like a young Chriftian;
and with fuch energy, that I cannot doubt
its fincerity. Perhaps if older Chriftians
than we were to come to a refolution to
break the fetters, to emancipate and kindly
raife up thefe poor afflicted fellow-crea-
tures, who are fo forely burthened, they
would feel a more exquifite fenfation than
they had ever before experienced.

A traveller relates, that " in walking
through a flave-yard, he faw a man about
thirty-five years old, in irons; he was a
a Mahometan, and could read and write
Arabic. He was occafionally noify; fometimes he would fing a melancholy fong,
then he would utter an earneft prayer,
and then perhaps would obferve a dead
filence." [This, by the way, I take to
be the very man whofe picture is here
exhibited.] " I afked the reafon of this
ftrange conduct, and learned that it was

in confequence of his ftrong feelings on
his having been juft put, for the firft time,
in irons. I believe he had begun to wear
them only the day before. As we paffed,
he cried aloud to us, and endeavoured to
hold up his irons to our view, which he
ftruck with his hand in a very expreffive
manner, the tear ftarting in his eye. He
feemed by his manner to be demanding
the caufe of his confinement.—How af-
fecting!—for a man in the prime of life
to be bound in irons, and perhaps doomed
to endure all the hardfhips and cruelties,
which it is well known are practifed upon
thefe poor men; and left to afk, perhaps
in vain, of the remorfelefs mafter, "What
is the caufe of this?—What has been my
crime? Wherein have I offended?"—
I truft there is not one of my young
readers whofe heart would not melt with
compaffion at the fight of this poor innocent fufferer, were they to fee him,
in a fupplicating pofture, with tears in
his eyes, calling out to them,

Am I not a Friend and a Brother?"

What an appeal to the human heart!—
Before I difmifs the fubject, you fhall have

a specimen of the *tenderness* of those men-
dealers.

"The captain of an American slave-
ship had lost a very fine slave; he died *of
the sulks*, as he emphatically termed it.
The following were his words, as near as
the person who related the fact could remember—" The man (he said) was a Mahometan, and uncommonly well made,
and it appeared to me, that he had been
some person of consequence. When he
first came on board, he was very much
cast down; but on finding that I allowed
him to walk at large, he got a little more
reconciled to the ship. When the number
of my slaves grew to be such that I could
not let them have their liberty any longer,
I put this man in irons like the rest, and
upon this his spirits sunk down again to such
a degree, that he never recovered it. He
complained of a *pain at his heart*, and would
not eat. The usual means were tried with
him, but it seemed all in vain, for he continued to reject food altogether, except
when I stood by him, and made him eat.
I left no method untried with him; for I
had set my heart on saving him. I am

perfuaded he would have brought me three hundred dollars in the Weft Indies; but nothing would fucceed. He faid from the firft he was determined to die, and accordingly fo he did, after lingering for the fpace of nine days. I affure you, Gentlemen, I felt very forry on the occafion, for I dare fay I loft three hundred dollars by his death; and, to fuch a man as me, that is a very heavy lofs!"

This is the compaffionate language of a flave-merchant. What muft this poor African have endured? Surely this was dying of grief—torn from all that was dear to him in life—he would have ftruggled with the miferable reverfe of his fortune with heroic fortitude—but chains—to laden an afflicted creature like this with chains—NO!—he *could not* bear that!—HE DIED!!!

> " Such, I exclaim, is the pitilefs part,
>   Some act by the delicate mind;
>   Regardlefs of wounding, or breaking a heart,
>   Already to forrow refign'd."

He without whofe permiffion " not a fparrow falls to the ground, and who feedeth the young ravens that call upon him,"

will not fuffer the meaneft work of his
hands to be treated cruelly with impu-
nity.   I remember fome moft beautiful
lines on this fubject written by that excellent poet, Cowper.   With his permiffion, I will borrow a few of them for your
gratification.

" Oh ! moft degrading of all ills that wait
On man, a mourner in his beft eftate !
All other forrows virtue may endure,
And find fubmiffion more than half a cure ;
Grief is itfelf a med'cine, and beftow'd
T"improve the fortitude that bears the load ;
To teach the wand'rer, as his woes increafe,
The path of Wifdom, all whofe paths are peace.
But Slav'ry ! Virtue dreads it, as her grave,
Patience itfelf is meannefs in the flave ;
Or if the will and fovereignty of God
Bid fuffer it a while, and kifs the rod,
Wait for the dawning of a brighter day,
And fnap the chain the moment when you may.
Oh! 'tis a godlike privilege to fave,
And he who fcorns it, is himfelf a flave.
*   *   *   *   *   *   *   *   *   *

A Briton knows, or if he knows it not,
The fcripture plac'd within his reach, he ought,
That fouls have no difcriminating hue,
Alike important in their Maker's view :
That none are free from blemifh fince the fall,
And Love Divine has paid one price for all.
                              C

The wretch that works, and weeps without relief,
Has one that notices his silent grief;
He from whose hands alone all power proceeds,
Ranks its abuse amongst the foulest deeds,
Considers *all* injustice with a frown,
But *marks* the man who treads his fellow down,
Remember, Heav'n has an avenging rod;
To smite the poor, is treason against God."

I believe the hour of rest draws nigh: we will therefore separate for the evening; bearing in our minds the sufferings which have been described, we shall not fail to commiserate the wretched, whilst we are rendered more truly sensible of the peculiar blessings bestowed upon us by the gracious hand of Providence.

THE THIRD EVENING.

ELDEST BOY.

OUR laſt evening's reading preſented us with a melancholy ſtory, and even excited our tears; I hope we may now find, by way of contraſt, ſomething pleaſant, to produce a ſmile, as the little elegant ſong ſays,

" The tear that is wip'd with a little addreſs,
" May be follow'd, perhaps, by a ſmile."

THE THIRD EVENING's READING.

INTEMPERANCE AND DISSIPATION.

The neareſt approach thou canſt make to happineſs on this ſide the grave, is to enjoy from heaven underſtanding and health. Theſe bleſſings if thou poſſeſſeſt, and wouldſt preſerve to old age, avoid the allurements of Voluptuouſneſs, and fly from her temptations.

C 2

When she spreadeth her delicacies on the board, when the wine sparkleth in the cup, when she smileth upon thee, and persuadeth thee to be joyful and happy; then is the hour of danger, then let Reason stand firmly on her guard; for if thou hearkenest unto the words of her adversary, thou art deceived and betrayed.

The joy which she promiseth, changeth to madness, and her enjoyments lead on to diseases and death.

————

I remember having met with a story, which shows the force of these observations.   I think it was called

THE TWO BEES.

On a fine morning in May, two bees set forward in queſt of honey; the one wiſe and temperate, the other careleſs and extravagant. They ſoon arrived at a garden enriched with aromatic herbs, the moſt fragrant flowers, and the moſt delicious fruits. They regaled themſelves for a time on the various dainties that were ſpread before them; the one loading his thighs at intervals with proviſions for the

C 3

hive againſt the diſtant winter, the other
revelling in ſweets, without regarding any
thing but preſent gratification. At length
they found a wide-mouthed phial, that
hung beneath the bough of a peach-tree,
filled with honey ready tempered, and ex-
poſed to their taſte in the moſt alluring
manner. The thoughtleſs epicure, in ſpite
of all his friend's remonſtrances, plunged
headlong into the veſſel, reſolving to indulge himſelf in all the pleaſures of ſenſu-
ality. The philoſopher, on the other hand,
ſipped a little with caution; but being
ſuſpicious of danger, flew off to fruits
and flowers; where, by the moderation
of his meals, he improved his reliſh for
the true enjoyment of them. In the evening, however, he called upon his friend,
to inquire whether he would return to the
hive, but found him ſurfeited in ſweets,
which he was as unable to leave, as to enjoy. Clogged in his wings, enfeebled in
his feet, and his whole frame totally ener-
vated; he was but juſt able to bid his
friends adieu, and to lament, with his
lateſt breath, that though a taſte of pleaſure might quicken the reliſh of life, an

unreftrained indulgence is inevitable deftruction.

————————

You will find the moral of this little
fable proved by daily experience, even
amongft yourfelves, my young friends;
the excefsive indulgence of your appetites
in fruits or fweets, or the too eager purfuit
of play or pleafure generally, if not always,
ends in remorfe. The former producing
loathing and ficknefs, prevents your application to your ftudies, and deprives you
of the real enjoyments intended for you
in the hours of recreation : the latter takes
up too great a portion of your time, diffi-
pates the mind, and equally renders you
unfit for application, whilft you are fuffering under the difpleafure of an offended tutor. Thefe are real evils to youth;
but they are only the beginning of forrows; if not timely checked, they will
grow up with you, increafe in ftrength,
and the diforder which at firft was painful and inconvenient, will in the end prove
deftructive. It is furprifing to behold
what infinitely various paths mankind take

in purfuit of pleafure, and yet how few
appear really to obtain it ; all are in full
cry after this will-o'-the-wifp—from the
all-accomplifhed Duchefs at a mafquerade,
to the little flirting heroine of a " baby
ball"———pell-mell they go !———

Who is fhe that with graceful fteps,
and with a lively air, trips over-yonder
plain ?

The rofe blufheth in her cheeks, the
fweetnefs of the morning breathes from
her lips ; joy, tempered with innocence
and modefty, fparkleth in her eyes, and
from the cheerfulnefs of her heart, fhe
fingeth as fhe walks !

Her name is HEALTH; fhe is the daughter of Exercife and Temperance ; their fons
inhabit the mountains of the northern re-
gions.

They are brave, active, and lively, and
partake of all the beauties of their filter.

Vigour ftringeth their nerves, ftrength
dwelleth in their bones, and labour is their
delight all the day long.

To combat the paffions is their delight ;
to conquer evil habits their glory.

Their pleasures are moderate, and therefore they endure; their repose is short, but sound and undisturbed——

Enter JONAS, *the Butler.*

Here is little Miss Lætitia Airy, call'd upon you, ladies and gentlemen.

O, desire her to walk in.

Enter Miss LÆTITIA.

O la, I am so happy to see you, how comfortably you are all set round the fire; I declare it's quite charming. For my part, I am an absolute slave; I have really no time for reading, or thinking, or walking, or sitting still, or any thing; I'm sure I shall be glad when this ball is over; but my 'ma has set her heart upon my making a figure there, and so has papa; and it's one's duty, I suppose, to please papa and mama, when one can, without doing any thing *very* disagreeable to one's selves, you know. I'm sure I have been six hours with Monsieur Molini, the French dancing-master, this day; but he gives me great encouragement; he says there is not any one young lady he has the honour to teach

who can stand on one toe so gracefully, or
for so long together.

LITTLE EDWARD.

Miss Letty, I should like to see you stand
upon one foot, and repeat the second
commandment.

LÆTITIA.

Lo, you little conceited thing, I know
nothing about commandments; 'Ma gives
particular orders that I am not to be commanded by any body, nor contradicted
neither; she says papa has plenty of money for me, and I shall do just as I please,
as long as I live.

EDWARD.

I don't believe she can repeat it, if she
stands upon both feet.

ELDEST BOY, *(aside to Edward.)*

That, brother Ned, is entirely *her mis-
fortune*, though perhaps not entirely her
fault, and it is not becoming in you to scoff
at the misfortunes of any one.—I would

not have you be offended at what little
Edward faid to you, Mifs Letty, he is but
a child. And though I really do think it
is a grievous thing for a young lady, nine
years old, not to be acquainted with *all
the ten commandmants*, yet there was fomething very improper in his behaviour on
the occafion.

LÆTITIA.

Nobody dare behave fo to me at home:
but, however, I muft be gone; I fee by my
watch it is near feven o'clock, and if I ftay
any longer, I fhall have dinner waiting for
me: and I muft not fit long over the wine
either; for, do you know, I fhall have an
alteration to make in my drefs for the
evening; we are going to have a party,
en famille, and there are to be feveral of
the officers of this new regiment, fo we
fhall be as gay as poffible.—Well adieu!
Bon jour—I'm forry to leave you fo foon;
but, really, *time is precious*.   [*Exit.*

ELDEST BOY.

Mifs Lætitia's fine fpeech ended with
a truth however; though, knowing the

value of this precious gift, time, she is moſt
exceedingly careleſs of it, I muſt confeſs.
We have great reaſon to rejoice, who can
reliſh "the ſimply joys and unbought delights" which ſurround us, without the
exceſſive fatigue poor Lætitia is forced to
endure in the attainment of her more
faſhionable pleaſures. She is exactly one
of thoſe Lilliputian coquettes mentioned
in that excellent book we ſaw upon the
table in father's library the other day. I
could not reſiſt copying out two or three
lines which ſtruck my fancy as I opened
it. I hope both my father and Miſs
Hannah More will forgive me if I have
done wrong :

"The true pleaſures of childhood are
cheap and natural; for every object teems
with delight to eyes and hearts new to the
enjoyment of life; nay, the hearts of
healthy children abound with a general
diſpoſition to mirth and joyfulneſs, even
without a ſpecific object to excite it;
like our firſt parent, in the world's firſt
ſpring, when all was new, and freſh, and
gay about him,

——————————"They live and move,
And feel that they are happier than they know."

This is a defcription of our little happy fociety. How thankful fhould we be for this peculiar happinefs, that God hath placed us under the care of parents who fee and provide for us the things belonging to our peace; and yet ftrew in our ways fo many innocent gratifications.

Mifs Lætitia is gone to dinner. It is fo long fince we have dined, that I fufpect it is almoft bed-time for moft of you, and time to retire for all. We clofed the book with fome very excellent fentences, let us bear them in our minds.

" Our pleafures are moderate, therefore they may endure; our repofe is fhort but found, and undifturbed."

D

THE FOURTH EVENING.

THE FOURTH EVENING's READING.

" OH Winter! ruler of th' inverted year,
Thy ſcatter'd hair with ſleet like aſhes fill'd,
Thy breath congeal'd upon thy lips, thy cheeks
Fring'd with a beard made white with other ſnows
Than thoſe of age ; thy forehead wrapt in clouds,
A leafleſs branch thy ſceptre, and thy throne
A ſliding car, indebted to no wheels,
But urg'd by ſtorms along its ſlipp'ry way,

I love thee, all unlovely as thou feem'ft,
And dreaded as thou art.

* * * * * * * * * * * *

I crown thee king of intimate delights,
Firefide enjoyments, home-born happinefs,
And all the comforts that the lowly roof
Of undifturb'd retirement, and the hours
Of long uninterrupted evening know.

* * * * * * * * * * * *

Come, Evening, once again, feafon of peace,
Return, fweet Evening, and continue long!"

ELDEST BOY.

Come, we open the evening's amufe
ment with a moft beautiful defcription of
fire-fide enjoyments; let us avail ourfelves
of thofe which now prefent themfelves.
We feem to be much more happily fitu-
ated than the poor old man in the picture
above; I wifh he was amongft us, he
feems half perifhed in the ftorm.

I am to inform you, that the fubjects
intended for the prefent evening, are,

SINCERITY AND TRUTH,

With their Oppofites.

" Sincerity and Truth form the bafis
of every virtue. That darknefs of charac-

D 2

ter, where we can fee no heart; thofe foldings of art, through which no native affection is allowed to penetrate, prefent an object, unamiable in every feafon of life, but particularly odious in youth. If, at an age when the heart is warm, when the emotions are ftrong, and when nature is expected to fhow herfelf free and open, you can already fmile and deceive, what are we to look for when you fhall be longer hackneyed in the ways of men. Diffimulation in youth is the fore-runner of perfidy in old age. Its firft appearance is the fatal omen of growing depravity and future fhame. It degrades parts and learning, obfcures the luftre of every accomplifhment, and finks you into contempt with God and man. As you value, therefore, the approbation of Heaven, or the efteem of the world, cultivate the love of truth. In all your proceedings be direct and confiftent. Ingenuity and candour poffefs the moft powerful charm; they befpeak univerfal favour, and carry an apology for almoft every failing. The path of truth is a plain and fafe path; that of falfehood is a perplexing maze. After the firft departure from fincerity, it is not in your power to ftop. One artifice unavoidably leads on to another, till, as the intricacy of the labyrinth increafes, you are left entangled in your own fnare. Deceit difcovers a little mind, which ftops at temporary expedients, without rifing to comprehenfive views of conduct. It is the refource of one who wants courage to avow his defigns, or to reft upon himfelf, whereas opennefs of character difplays that generous boldnefs which ought to diftinguifh youth.

"To fet out in the world with no other principle than a crafty attention to intereft, betokens one who is deftined for creeping through the inferior walks of life; but to give an early preference to honour above gain, when they ftand in competition; to defpife every advantage which cannot be attained without difhoneft arts; to brook no meannefs, and to ftoop to no diffimulation, are the indications of a *great mind*, the prefages of future eminence, and diftinction in life. At the fame time, this virtuous fincerity is perfectly confiftent with the moft prudent vigilance and cau-

D 3

tion. It is oppofed to cunning, not to true
wifdom. It is not the fimplicity of a weak
and improvident, but the candour of an
enlarged and noble-mind; of one who
fcorns deceit, becaufe he accounts it both
bafe and unprofitable, and who feeks no
difguife, becaufe he needs none to hide
him."

So preaches the admirable Blair; and I
pray, my young friends, that you may
bring thofe valuable precepts into practice.

I fhall endeavour to amufe you by a
ftory, the fubject of a little drama, in the
works of M. Berquin; with an intent to
fhow that thofe who are walking in the
paths of error and deceit are fure, fooner
or later, to be caught in their own fnare.

HONESTY IS THE BEST POLICY.

The Countefs of D. had invited Harry
and Eliza, a nobleman's younger fon, and
his daughter, to pafs the day at her houfe
with her own children, Auguftus and Julia,
together with Gabriel, Lucian, and Flora,
three friends who lived in the neighbourhood.

In the absence of the Countess, this young party had got possession of several dozens of silver counters, which were highly valued by the Countess, and her orders had been peremptorily given, that her children should not have them to play with. Master Harry, however, got hold of them; and, in spite of all that Julia could say, who offered at the same time her own ivory ones, he would have them out to play with, telling her they always had as good, or better at home. He took them himself out of the drawer; and having thrown them about the room, and behaved in a very rude, unbecoming manner for some time, he proposed going to play in the garden.

Rachel, one of the servants, passing through the room where they had been playing, was astonished to see her lady's valued counters thrown about. She gathered them up; and, in order to prevent all mistakes, counted them over and over again, but could only make fifty-four—there ought, she knew, to be five dozen—six were wanting. Rachel was greatly concerned at this accident, and expected

to be blamed by her lady, at leaft as being
accefary in giving them out. The Countefs enters, afks the caufe of her uneafi-
nefs, and is told of the lofs of the fix counters. At this time Julia enters the room:
the Countefs is angry with her for taking
out the counters; when, with a compofure
and artlefs fimplicity which proved her
own innocence, fhe related the facts which
have been ftated concerning them. The
maid fufpected fome of the young vifitors,
and recommended that Mafter's pockets
fhould be examined. The Countefs re-
proved her for the thought of offering
fuch an affront to their parents as that
would be, and Julia endeavoured to ex-
culpate the whole party. The ftricteft
fearch was made, but none of the fix
counters could be found. Adam, a faith-
ful old fervant, is called into court; but
he can give no account of them; he has
not feen them. After fome deliberation,
however, Adam undertakes to find the
thief: provided he might have leave to
put his own plan in execution, he had no
doubt of producing the counters. The
Countefs, knowing his prudence, at length

confented to this; and Adam went to get his conjuring fticks and other matters ready.

The young family were all affembled together, when Adam's experiment was to be made. It may not be amifs to give the fhort fcene of the drama which precedes the examination.

SCENE III.

THE QUARREL!

The Countefs. Well, how fares it with you all, my little friends? I am glad to fee you here.

Harry. Mifs Julia has juft now informed us you have loft fix counters of the number we unluckily were playing with. I'm forry for it; but could never thing your Ladyfhip would have fufpected that one of us had taken them. At leaft I can affure you for my fifter and myfelf, that we know nothing of them.

The Countefs. I could not poffibly fufpect fuch well-bred children. Sure Julia did not fay I fufpected you.

Eliza. No, my Lady, all she said was to inquire if we had brought them out through inattention.

The Countefs. Which you might very innocently have done.

Lucian. I would never dare to fhow my face again, if I had taken even a pin.

Flora (emptying her pockets.) See, my Lady, I have nothing.

The Countefs. My dear children, I have already told you I am far from thinking any of you have them, when you fay you have not. They are certainly of no great value; yet I cannot but confefs their lofs affects me.

Harry. Were they only worth a ftraw, they were your Ladyfhip's, and fhould not now be miffing. But you know there are fuch things as fervants, and they are not always honeft. 'Tis not the firft time we have fufpected them at home.

Julia. But 'tis the firft time any thing of the kind has happened in our houfe, I affure you, Mafter Harry.

Auguftus. I would anfwer for our fervants, men and women.

The Countefs. I have trufted them this

long time; but if you, Sir, *(to Harry)* have made any obfervations, I requeft you'd let me know them.

Harry. Oh, no, no! But when we went into the garden, did not what's her name, the houfe-maid, enter?

The Countefs. Rachel! oh, I don't fear her. Thefe fix years paft that I have I had her, fhe might eafily have made away with things of value, had fhe been difhoneft.

Harry. Did not your old footman come in likewife? I don't like his looks.

The Countefs. Fie, Sir! What makes you thus fufpect the honeft Adam? He was my father-in-law's confidential fervant, and has been much longer in the family than I myfelf.

Harry. 'Tis not unlikely, then, that fome one may have got into the room when we were gone.

The Countefs. That's not at all unlikely; and I am going to inquire. Amufe yourfelves till I come back.

Harry. No, Madam, after what has paffed, I cannot ftay any longer here. Auguftus, can you tell me where they have put my hat?

The Countess. I can't let you possibly
go home on foot. You wou'd have up-
wards of three miles to walk. Stay here
till I return ; I wont detain you long.
You know your papa means to come and
fetch you in the carriage.   *(Exit.*

Harry. I'm very much astonished your
mamma should have such thoughts of us !
We steal her counters !

Julia. Neither has she such a thought.
She might have fancied we had put them,
without thought, into our pockets. But,
as you say, *steal,* she did not think of such
a word, or any like it.

Harry. Had there been none here but
tradesmen's children, she might well have
entertained suspicions ; but should make
some difference now.

Gabriel. You speak of us, Sir, I can
see. Your looks inform me so ; but let
me tell you, in my turn, that 'tis one's
way of living, and not birth, one should
be proud of, if they are proud at all.

Harry. How these tradesmen talk about
their way of living. You are very happy
there are so few children hereabout, and
that Augustus and myself are forced to

make you our companions, or have no di-
verſion. Did you live in London, you
would not have ſuch an honour, notwith-
ſtanding your fine way of living.

Auguſtus. Speak, Sir, for yourſelf alone:
for juſt as here, in London too, I ſhould
be proud to entertain my little friends.

Julia. Yes, certainly, they give us, to
the full, as good examples as ſuch
whipper-ſnapper noblemen as you.

Eliza. This, brother, you have deſerved.
Why firſt attack them?

Harry. And you, too, upon me? You
think certainly as I do, though you wont
confeſs you do. Have you forgot mamma's
inſtruction on the ſubject of familiarity
with thoſe beneath us? "Never mix with
tradeſmen's children; in the lower ranks
of life you'll always have low thoughts."

Auguſtus. And can you poſſibly ſuſpect
my friends of being *thieves?*

Gabriel. Did we approach the table?

Flora. No; whereas we ſaw you take
the counters, and look at them half a
dozen times. *(Harry aims to ſtrike her.)*

Auguſtus. Softly! you'll have me to
deal with elſe.

E

Gabriel. No, no, my friend, I thank you, but I can take care of my fifter.

Harry. O 'tis far beneath me to difpute with traders.

Julia. Very well; I hope then it is beneath you likewife to attack a little girl.

Harry. I fha'nt permit her to infult me.

Eliza. She certainly would have done much better, had fhe held her tongue.

Julia. But being fuch a child, fhe might be pardoned; and particularly when fhe fpoke the truth.

Harry. The truth?

Gabriel. Yes, if you underftood that word. She faid you took the counters and looked at them, and this certainly was true.

Harry. I fha'nt even condefcend to anfwer you.

Gabriel. You can't take a better refolution, when you have nothing but fuch anfwers for us.

———

By this time the Countefs returns, and invites them into an adjoining room, where Adam is prepared for his experiment. Adam introduces a cock, which, he tells them is a conjurer. He fets down the

baſket on the table, and lifts up a napkin
which was covered over it, ſo that Flora
and the reſt diſcerned the creature's neck
and creſt, informing them, that if a ſingle
ſtraw is miſſing, he need only conſult this
bird, and he will be ſure to know who
ſtole it. Adam now cloſes in all the win-
dows—all is darkneſs. He now addreſſes
them as follows: If any one is guilty of
ſtealing the counters, let him go out—
What, all remain! Come, then, Gentlemen and Ladies, and let every one of you
in turn, lift up the napkin here, and with
his right hand, d'ye ſee, ſtroke Chanti-
clear upon his back, you will hear his muſic the moment the thief lays his hand
upon him; but don't lift the cloth too
high; juſt ſo as to let your hand paſs under it.

They all ſeverally comply with the command, each exclaiming, "It is not I; the
cock don't ſpeak"—Harry declaring he had
ſtroked him more than the reſt, and he did
not even ſpeak for him. Adam places
the company in a row, with their right
hands behind them, as each paſſes the table.
The whole company now having paſſed
the trial, a general laugh, in which the

Countefs joins, is directed againft poor
Adam and the conjurer.——I muft acknowledge this confounds me, fays Adam.
However, have patience for a little while
don't ftir; be fure to ftand ftill. There
muft be fomething wrong, I'll go fetch a
candle.—Harry knew what all this ftupid
nonfenfe would come to. Flora fufpected
the cock was no wifer than his mafter.
Adam, returning with the light, goes
up to Flora : " Come, Mifs, let me fee
your right hand " She holds out her right
hand. All are greatly furprifed to find
it as black as a coal. " Don't be frightened,
little Mifs, I'll foon make it white again."
The children have no patience, but look
all together at their hands, and inftantly
cry out, " How black are my fingers too !"
After much furprife, and many remarks
having been made on this phænomenon,
Harry lifts up his hand in triumph, exclaiming, " But fee mine ! there's none
but I have got a hand that's fit to look at."
" Very likely !" fays Adam, taking hold
of Harry by the collar, " 'tis then *you* have
ftole the counters ! Give them up, young
gentleman, this inftant, or I'll fearch your
pockets, and then black you all over."

Harry (turning pale and trembling.) Is it poffible I fhould have put them in my pocket, and not thought of what I was about? I recollect, indeed, I had them in my hand. Dear me! they're here indeed, in a corner of my pocket! Who would have thought it?"—He begins to invent excufes—it was done without confideration—he is charged with not having touched the cock—he declares he *did* ftroke it.

Countefs. "You *did*; is that then your affertion? Don't you fee, that if you had, you would have blacked your hands, as all the others, Adam having fmeared him over with a certain compofition. Your companions were not the leaft afraid to ftroke him, as their confcience did not any way reproach them for the theft; but as for you, the apprehenfion you were under, that the fervant's artifice might really be conjuration, awed you; and the means you pitched on to avoid detection have betrayed you. You thought yourfelf very *politic*, no doubt, in *pretending* only, as you did, to ftroke the cock—but HONESTY you would have found much better POLICY!"

Being thus pinned down by the evidence againſt him, he confeſſes the crime.

ELDEST BOY.

What a pretty figure the little nobleman makes in this hiſtory! Let us charitably hope there are not *many* children educated in this crooked way. What a depraved mind is here deſcribed! What pride! What meanneſs!—Surely it would be more deſirable to be brought up in the pooreſt cottage, and afterwards to work hard at ſome low trade, and earn one's bread by their daily labour, rather than be a ſpoil'd child in high life, and afterwards a little nobleman turned looſe into ſociety to ſow the ſeeds of diſcord.

We have ſeen the vice of inſincerity painted in ſuch odious colours, that if our hearts had not been already ſet againſt it, the picture alone would have been enough to have fixed in us an hatred of the original.

I believe we muſt cloſe the buſineſs of the evening; for to-morrow we have a long, and ſeemingly, intereſting portion: let us meet early.

THE FIFTH EVENING.

ELDEST BOY.

THE subject for the present evening is a serious one, and well deserves our earnest consideration. It opens I perceive, in the manner of a sermon, I must therefore request that silence may be preserved; and, that such of you as are old enough to understand, will listen, with the strictest attention, to a short discourse

ON THE CHOICE OF COMPANIONS.

THE FIFTH EVENING's READING.

" Evil communications corrupt good manners."

Doubtless all people suffer from such communication; but, above all, the minds of youth suffer, which are yet unformed,

unprincipled, unfurnifhed, and ready to receive any impreffion.

Before we confider the danger of bad
company, let us fee the meaning of the
phrafe.

In the language of the world, *good company* means *fafhionable people;* their ftations
in life, not their morals, are confidered.
I fhould wifh you to fix another meaning
to the expreffion, to confider all company
in which vice is found, be their ftation
what it will, as bad company.

The three following claffes will perhaps
include the greateft part of thofe who de-
ferve the appellation.

Firft, thofe who endeavour to deftroy
the principles of Chriftianity; who jeft
upon fcripture, talk blafphemy, and treat
revelation with contempt.

A fecond clafs, thofe who have a tendency to deftroy in us the principles of
common honefty and integrity. Under
this head we may rank gamefters of every
denomination, and the infamous characters
of every profeffion.

A third clafs, and fuch as are commonly
moft dangerous to youth, includes the

long catalogue of men of pleasure. In whatever way they follow the call of appetite, they have equally a tendency to corrupt the purity of the mind. Besides these three classes, whom we may call *bad* company, there are others who come under the denomination of *ill-chosen* company; trifling, insipid characters of every kind, who follow no business, are led by no ideas of improvement, but spend their time in dissipation and folly; whose highest praise it is, that they are not vicious. With none of these a serious youth would wish to associate.

The danger of keeping bad company, arises, principally, from our aptness to imitate and catch the manners and sentiments of others; from the power of custom; and from our own bad inclinations.

In our earliest youth, the contagion of manners is observable. In a child we easily discover, from his first actions, and rude attempts at language, the kind of persons to whose care he has been committed: we see the early spring of a civilized education, or the first wild shoots of rusticity. In childhood and youth, we naturally adopt the sentiments of thofe about us.

Habit, which is intended for our good, may, like other kind appointments of nature, be converted into a mifchief. The well-difpofed youth, entering firft into bad company, is fhocked at what he hears and what he fees. The good principles he has imbibed, ring in his ears an alarming leffon againft the wickednefs of his companions. But, alas! this fenfibility is but of fhort continuance. The horrid picture is now more eafily endured,

" Vice is a creature of fo horrid mien,
As to be hated, needs but to be feen;
Yet feen too oft, familiar to her face,
We firft endure—then pity—then embrace."

Virtue is foon thought a fevere rule; the gofpel an inconvenient reftraint; a few pangs of confcience now and then interrupt his pleafures, and whifper to him that he once had better thoughts: but even thefe die away; and he who at firft was fhocked even at the appearance of vice, is formed by cuftom into a profligatd leader of vicious pleafures.

Our bad inclinations form another argument againſt bad company. We have ſo many bad propenſities of different kinds to watch, that, amidſt ſuch a variety of enemies within, we ought at leaſt to be on our guard againſt thoſe without. It is therefore the part of inexperienced youth, ſurely, to keep out of the way of temptation, and to give bad inclinations as little room as poſſible to acquire ſtrength.

It is very true, and a lamentable faɛt; in the hiſtory of human nature, that bad men take more pains to corrupt their own ſpecies, than virtuous men do to reform them.

I ſhall now proceed to a ſhort ſtory, which applies to our ſubjeɛt, and is adapted to the underſtandings of the younger part of my readers.

This ſtory has never before appeared in print; it is well worth your attention, and I hope you will none of you loſe a word of it.

STORY OF MASTER TRUEMAN.

MASTER TRUEMAN was the ſon of a reſpeɛtable tradeſman, who lived at a ſmall diſtance from the metropolis. He

was an only child; and his parents, who
were very confcientious people, and poffeffed confiderable property, were, as it
may be fuppofed, extremely anxious for
the welfare of this boy. He went to a
fchool in the neighbourhood, the mafter
of which was an elderly clergyman, a very
pious man, and in all refpects, an ex-
emplary character. This boy, whom we
fhall now diftinguifh by the name of Edmund, poffeffed a good natural under-
ftanding, was a dutiful and affectionate
child; and by his general good conduct,
had rendered himfelf the delight of his
parents' hearts.

During the fchool hours he was always
attentive to his bufinefs, and feldom re-
turned home without fome peculiar marks
of approbation, having been beftowed on
him by his mafter.

His evenings ufed to be fpent in pre-
paring his tafk for the morning, in reading fome ufeful and amufing book, in
drawing, or fome other rational employment, during the Winter. And in the
Summer he would walk in the fields with
his father and mother, and fometimes

perhaps a neighbour; and though only ten years of age, he would speak of the beauties of nature, and attempt to trace the finger of God in all that presented itself to his view, with so much good sense, that he at once delighted and astonished those who heard him.

There happened to be in this school (which consisted of only twelve boys,) two or three youths, who did not exactly walk in Edmund's steps; but then they were adepts at every sport and pastime which came in with the different seasons.—Though they were perpetually turned back at their lessons, and could not be taught to join two letters decently together with their pen; yet none were more expert in flying a kite, playing at shoe and ball, skipping through the rope, and so forth, in the summer; or at skating, sliding, throwing snow-balls, and such sort of sports, in the winter. These were very *alluring* qualifications, and they were in themselves harmless; but unhappily here they served to cover a very bad disposition. Those boys were constantly playing the truant, robbing gardens, and one of them,

F

Richard Humphreys, in particular, had
been detected more than once in such acts
as stealing the boys' knives and books, and
felling them; but this was not generally
known in the school. In short, fome of
them were continually under punifhment
for one crime or other; but then, when
fchool was over, they had fo many feducing
ways, and could make themfelves fo very
agreeable, that it was fcarcely poffible for
any one to avoid their fociety, and from
joining in thofe fports wherein they fo
greatly excelled, particularly one whofe
heart was good, who meant only to partake of fuch fports as were innocent, and
even thofe only at proper times.

One morning as Edmund was trudging
to fchool in the ufual way, he was met by
Richard Humphreys, who joined him, and
turned back part of the way with him.
" A fine morning, Mafter Edmund," fays
Dick; " you are going to fchool, I perceive." Edmund anfwered in the affirma-
tive. " For my part, I am going to a village hard by; there is a mountebank to
exhibit, and they fpeak very highly of the
merry Andrew, who, they fay, is the moft

witty fellow, and has the clevereſt tricks of any one that ever appeared upon a ſtage."

" I ſhould like very well to ſee him," ſays Edmund; " if it had happened to have been a holiday, I would have aſked my father's permiſſion to go and ſee him."

" Beſides," adds Richard, " I have got a ſhilling in my pocket, and I know of a boy who won a ſilver watch the other day by putting a ſhilling into the mountebank's lottery, where they ſay there are not any blanks. I intend to try my luck to-day."

" I ſhould like to go" ſays Edmund, " but it would be a ſin and a ſhame to neglect ſchool; beſides I ſhould be too late, was I to go back to aſk leave." " Why, truly," replies Richard, " it would be a ſhameful thing indeed to miſs ſchool *often* in this way, but a *time by chance*—it is only two hours—I think there can be no very great harm in doing this *for once* in one's life. We can ſoon make up, by a little extraordinary application, for the loſs of two hours, and we ſhall be back by the dinner-hour, ſo that no one need know any thing of the matter; one may eaſily

invent fome excufe to the mafter, and
then all is over."

At this time who fhould come up but
Tom Laurence and Billy Bentill, two intimate friends of Richard's, (for this, you
muft know, was a concerted plan)—thefe
boys had long been difgufted by the attention of the mafter to Edmund, and his
ill treatment, as they termed it, of them;
they were determined to bring matters a
little on a level, not by mending their own
ways, and copying Edmund's conduct,
which in their hearts they could not help
approving, but by endeavouring to pervert
his fteps, and, by entangling him in their
bafenefs, bring him, by degrees, to be as
infamous as themfelves. This is very common with bad children; as it is much eafier
for an artful lad to make a well-difpofed
boy as bad as himfelf, provided he affo-
ciates much with them, than it is for him
to wean himfelf from all his vicious habits,
and, by conftant imitation, bring himfelf
to be as good as he found his companion;
this is often attended with a great deal of
trouble, and requires much perfeverance.
But to go on with the ftory. Tom and

Billy coming up, one of them, addreffing Dick Humphreys, afked what he was about loitering there; every body was gone! they fhould be too late if they did not run: for their parts, they would not be too late for all the world. "Come, Edmund," fays Richard, "'tis but for once, let us take a run with them; you would never forgive yourfelf, if you were to mifs the fight, and this is the laft time of performing." Here was not one moment left for reflection— now or never.—Edward's heart throbbed with the defire of feeing this fcene of mirth and jollity; away they run together, nor do they relax their pace until they reach the village. This was an unlucky meeting, indeed, to poor Edmund. As they ftood laughing at the Merry Andrew and his jokes, Richard pretended to be greatly concerned all of a fudden. At length he exclaims, "Alas! alas! I have loft my fhilling; I put it into my waiftcoat pocket to be ready, and, in the violence of running, it has flown out. [*The truth is, he had no fhilling to lofe.*] If you, mafter Edmund, would be fo kind as lend me one, I will promife you part of what I fhall gain

by it." "Aye," say the other lads, "and
if you will lend each of us one, we will
do the same." "I have only two shillings
in my pocket," says Edmund; "which I
was taking to school for my contribution
towards coals for our fire. [*Here a sad
thought glanced across his mind.*] I will venture to lend you one of them, Richard, and
the other to your friends; but the only
condition I make is, that you will pay the
money again, that it may be appropriated
to the purpose for which I received it."
These terms were readily acceded to, and
the tickets were purchased. Now, big
with expectation and hope, the three ad-
venturers lost all relish for the jokes of the
fool; anxiety for the fate of their tickets
took entire possession of them. Edmund
continued to be amused for a little time,
when the tickets were both declared to be
blanks; the Merry Andrew at the same
time assuring them, that the two packets
were worth their weight in gold; these,
however, they soon found were of no more
value than a small quantity of brick-dust.
The money was gone! the time was gone!
and never was more solemnity seen than

in a fad proceffion of the four forrowful
lads, from the fcene of mirth, to the place
of retribution.

In order to fcreen the proceedings of
the morning, it now became neceffary, as
they thought, to invent as many lies and
falfe excufes as might be deemed expedi-
ent to effect that purpofe. This, in their
walk home, they contrived by the affiftance of Richard, who was an adept in this
fort of bufinefs, the affair was fo artfully
managed, that no part of the tranfaction
was brought to light.

When the evening came, Edmund was
obferved not to be fo cheerful as ufual;
his parents were uneafy, and thought he
could not poffibly be well, as he had always
been the life of their little fociety, till the
hour of his retiring. He complained of
a flight head-ach, though, if he had given
his diforder the right name, he would
have called it the *heart*-ache; for truly he
fuffered much remorfe. He went foon to
bed, but not to fleep; his heart fmote him
for his paft mifconduct; he felt himfelf de-
bafed; and could not find a place where
his head would reft eafy, all the night.

He arose early next day; the morning
was clear and fine; the air was fresh and
bracing; his spirits revived; he went to
school; all passed smoothly on, and he be-
gan to think more lightly of the excursion
to the neighbouring village.   The fact is,
he had been tempted to set his foot over the
boundary line of discretion; the act had
passed off unnoticed, and it is ten to one,
but on the next temptation, the other foot
will follow.   It was not long, indeed, before this happened.   There came a very
hard frost, and the river, which they frequently touched upon in their road to
school was frozen over, so that people
might, with discretion, walk over it with
a tolerable degree of safety.   As Edmund
set off to school one morning, Mr. Trueman said to him, "My dear Edmund,
you will oblige me, by not going upon the
ice in your way to school; so many acci-
dents happen from boys venturing without
a guide, that I shall really be quite unhappy
until I have your promise, that you will
avoid it.   To-morrow, you know, is a
holiday, and you shall go and walk there
with me; if the frost continue, as it is

likely to do, we may then more fafely venture. Edmund promifed he would not come near the ice; and with this refolution he fet off to fchool. There was a fudden bend in the river, which brought it fo near the foot path acrofs the lawn, that it gave you a full view of it to a great extent.

It was a fine winter's morning: the fun fhone on the ice, and exhibited a number of people who were fkating upon the river, in a part where the water was known to be fhallow. Here bonfires were made on the ice, hot ale and cakes were feen in various fituations; fome perfons were fliding, others engaged in various fports; all feemed gay, all were delighted. At this unlucky moment, with a fine fweep of their fkates, up came Richard Humphreys and his two companions. Edmund had never had a pair of fkates on; it was beautiful to fee people fkate, they did it with fo much eafe, and fome fo gracefully. "Try mine on," fays Humphreys; "you are very welcome; I'm fure you'll foon learn." "I fhould not be able to ftand up in them, I fear; befides, I would not be feen upon the ice juft at this time; I

have a reafon for it," "O, if that be all,
come along with me, I'll conduct you to a
place where there will be nobody but
ourfelves." So far Humphreys faid right;
for in that place the water was fo very
deep, that no prudent perfon, in the prefent ftate of the froft, would venture upon
it. Edmund fuffered himfelf once more
to be enticed by this artful companion.
Humphreys took off his fkates, and having
arrived at the folitary place of appoint-
ment, fixed them upon Edmund's feet,
and led him about, till he could ftand up-
right alone, and foon after move along
from place to place. He had however no
power of directing himfelf with certainty,
but was run away with, firft in one direc-
tion, then in another, whilft Humphreys
was fliding backwards and forwards on the
place where Edmund had fet off. An unlucky turn at length carried him to a hole
which had been broken open for the purpofe of getting water; down he fell into
the deep hole! His right arm caught the
edge of the ice, and had any one been
near, they might have dragged him out.
He cried out moft lamentably! Humphreys

difcovers his fituation. "Aye, very likely," fays he to himfelf, "fhall I go to
expofe my life, and afterwards get nothing
but abufe from his friends? not I, I'll run
off; find him out that can, mum's the
word for me." Away he ran! leaving
his companion, the unhappy victim of his
own credulity. If Humpreys had gone
and called for affiftance, the youth might
yet have been faved; but that was not for
his purpofe, he was determined not to be
feen in the bufinefs.

Mr. Aimworth, the fchoolmafter, however, not reconciled to Edmund's abfent-
ing himfelf from his duty a fecond time,
fent to know the caufe of his abfence. Mr.
Trueman, greatly alarmed at this meffage,
ran out, half diftracted; the ice immediately occurred to him, and he knew not
how far the temptation might have proved
refiftible; his fears, alas! were too well
grounded. Mafter Edmund had not been
feen by any one on the river; no body
could give any account of him. A decent,
elderly farmer happened to be looking
about his concerns in the fold-yard, and
him they queftioned.

This farmer had feen two boys at a little
diftance, running towards the river down
below; one of them appeared to have a
pair of fkates in his hands, but his eye-
fight was not very good, he could not con-
jecture what boys they might be. But
feeing the affliction of Mr. Trueman, and
the extreme concern of the meffenger; for
every body loved little Edmund, he offered
to go with them in fearch of this ill-fated

little boy. They came at length to the
dreadful fpot; here were footfteps of two
people to be traced on the fnow, (which

had not been fwept away for reafons before mentioned,) and the irregular marks of a pair of fkates were alfo traced to the broken part of the ice. The father's heart now funk within him—he had loft his all!— his only hope, his darling child was loft! was gone for ever!—his senses forfook him—he fell down upon the ice.

Farmer Heartwell, for that was the good old man's name, was ftruck by the appearance of fomething he did not per-fectly comprehend. He left Mr True-man to the care of the young man who accompanied him, whilft he endeavoured to account for a cavity which appeared to have been recently made in the hedge, alfo for the fnow being confiderably dif-turbed on that fide of the hole next to the hedge. He goes to the other fide, into a clofe adjoining the river. The fa-ther at this time recovers, and as they raife him up from the ice, he hears Far-mer Heartwell cry out, with a tranfport little fhort of madnefs, " He's here! I've found him! I have him!"

But oh! What language can defcribe the fcene, when he bears young Edmund

G

to his father's arms! pale, and shivering
indeed, but, evidently, in a state of reco-
very. A Newfoundland dog belonging
to a gentleman in the neighbourhood
came up to them shaking his tail; it seems
he had been strolling that way, and coming near to the scene of distress, seized
Edmund by the arm, just as he was sink-
ing, and drew him, nearly exhausted,
out of the water.

The sequel of my history is as follows:
Edmund is taken home, and soon re-

covers; this check which he has received from the arm of Divine Providence, opens his eyes fully to the danger of bad company; he repents, reforms, and is forgiven. Humphreys is charged with tempting him to go upon the ice; he denies the charge, and fays he was not on the ice that day. Farmer Heartwell obferves that the left foot of one of the perfons who had been there, from the impreffions left on the thin fnow which covered the ice, was turned inwards, and exactly anfwered to a deformity in that of Humphreys! befides, the fkates which Edmund had on were marked R. H. He is proved guilty; and, continuing in his bad habits, (for he never would confefs his fault, nor acknowledge the truth, but, in fpite of all remonftrance, went on from crime to crime,) he was at length fhunned and avoided by all who were not as bafe as himfelf.

I fhall forbear making any comments on this little ftory. It is brought here to fhow you the dreadful confequences which may arife from affociating with wicked companions; and I hope it has placed the danger so full to your view, that you will not " walk in the way of the evil man," but " avoid it; pass not by it; turn from " it, and pass away."

ELDEST BOY.

I never read any thing which left a stronger impression upon my mind than the subjects of this evening. O, my little friends and brothers, never let them be forgotten. At present, indeed, we are protected from bad company, we do not mix even with the *little world*, but live in our own select society; the time may come, when we must issue forth into the *great world*; let us remember that the enemy of mankind is constantly going about, assuming every shape to allure and insnare the virtuous; and we see plainly, that the best of us may fall into his hands, if we are not as constantly on our guard.

THE SIXTH EVENING.

ELDEST BOY.

WELCOME once more, my little friends, to the enjoyment of the retired fire-fide, and rational amufement.

We open the bufinefs of the night with another ferious fubject,

THE EMPLOYMENT OF TIME.

You are here prefented with the figure of an old man, fleeting along upon wings, bearing an hour-glafs in one hand, and a

G 3

scythe in the other. This old gentleman
holds his glafs up to us, I fuppofe, to re-
mind us, that as fwiftly as he flies, fo
fwiftly is the fand of the hour-glafs of our
lives pafling away; and the fcythe feems
to denote, that he means to mow us all,
down, before he has done with us. A few
fcattered ruins which appear behind him,
fhow what devaftation he makes; and the
darknefs which furrounds him, intimates
to us, that he can travel as faft by night
as by day. What is to be done with this
formidable perfonage? Let us take him
by the forelock; if we cannot check him
in his career, we will at leaft make him
ufeful to us, as we fly along with him.

————" Arrefi the prefent moments;
For be affur'd they all are arrant tell tales;
And though their flight be filent, and their path
Tracklefs, as the wing'd couriers of the air,
They poft to Heav'n, and there record our folly."

THE SIXTH EVENING's READING.

ON THE EMPLOYMENT OF TIME,

Its Use and Value.

Nothing is more common, than to hear people complain of the shortness of Time; and yet how much more have most of us than we make a proper use of, and many of us than we know how to use at all. " Our lives," says Seneca, " are spent either in doing nothing at all, or doing nothing to the purpose, or in doing nothing that we ought to do. We are always complaining our days are few, and acting as though there would be no end of them."

Yet as fast as our time runs, we should be very glad, in many parts of our lives, that it ran much faster than it does. This seems extraordinary, when we consider, that, notwithstanding the *business* of life, there are so many amusements to fill up the spaces of time. The mind, indeed, cannot be always intent on serious application; it is necessary therefore, to find out proper employments for it in its relaxations. " I must confess I think it is below reasonable creatures to be altogether

converfant in fuch diverfions as are merely innocent, and have nothing elfe to re-
commend them but that there is no hurt
in them. It is wonderful to fee perfons
of the beft fenfe pafling away a dozen
hours together in fhuffling and dividing a
pack of cards, with no other converfation
but what is made up of a few game
phrafes, and no other ideas, but thofe of
black or red fpots, ranged together in
different figures." Thus putting themfelves on the level, or perhaps fuffering
themfelves to be overcome by men of the
weakeft underftandings: for it is remarkable, however obftrufe the fcience of card-
playing may feem, perfons of the meaneft
capacity have been known to excel in it.
Would not one laugh to hear people of
this fpecies complain of the fhortnefs of
life, whilft they are calling to their aid,
cards,

———————————" With all the tricks
That idlenefs has ever yet contriv'd
To fill the void of an unfurnifh'd brain,
To palliate Dulnefs, and give Time a fhove."

The mind never unbends itfelf fo agree-
ably as in the converfation of a well-chofen
friend; this eafes and unloads it; clears

and improves the underſtanding; engenders thought and knowledge; and animates virtue and good reſolution.

There are many uſeful amuſements of life which one would endeavour to multiply, that one might always have recourſe to ſomething, rather than ſuffer the mind to lie idle, or run adrift with any paſſion that chances to riſe in it.

A perſon who has a taſte in muſic, painting, or architecture, is like one that has another ſenſe, when compared with ſuch as have no reliſh for thoſe arts. The floriſt, the planter, the gardener, the huſbandman, the turner, or he that employs himſelf at the anvil, when theſe are only as accompliſhments to the man of fortune, are great reliefs to a country life, and many ways uſeful to thoſe who are poſſeſſed of them.

" How various his employments whom the world
Calls idle, and who juſtly, in return,
Eſteems that buſy world an idler too!
Friends, books, a garden, and perhaps a pen,
Delightful induſtry enjoy'd at home,
And nature in her cultivated trim
Dreſs'd to his taſte, inviting him abroad."

But, inaſmuch as it behoveth perſons in every ſituation of life to conſider that they were not created to to live for themselves alone, they should " take care to keep their confcience peculiarly alive to the unapparent, though formidable perils of unprofitablenefs."

It is necefsary to habituate our minds, in our younger years, to fome employment which may engage our thoughts, and fill the capacity of the foul at a riper age. For, however we may roam in youth from folly to folly, too volatile for reft, too foft and effeminate for induftry, ever ambitious to make a fplendid figure, yet the time will come when we fhall outgrow the relifh of childifh amufements ; and, if we are not provided with a tafte for manly fatisfactions to fucceed in their room, we muft of courfe become miferable, at an age more difficult to be pleafed.

Frivolous excufes for not attending to ferious employments, are whimfically imagined by Mrs. Chapone, who fuppofing a modern lady of fafhion to be called to account for the difpofition of her time, makes her defence run thus:

" I can't, you know, be out of the world, nor act differently from every body in it. The hours are every where

late, confequently I rife late. I have
fcarce breakfafted before morning vifits
begin, or 'tis time to go to an auction, or
a concert, or to take a little exercife for my
health. Dreffing my hair is a long opera-
tion, but one can't appear with a head un-
like every body elfe. One muft fometimes
go to a play or an opera, though I own it
hurries one to death. Then what with
indifpenfable vifits, the perpetual engage-
ments to card-parties at private houfes,
and attendance on public affemblies, to
which all people of fafhion fubfcribe, the
evenings, you fee, are fully difpofed of.
What time, then, can I poffibly have for
what you call domeftic duties? You talk
of the offices and employments of friendfhip—alas! I have no hours left for friends!
I muft fee them in a crowd, or not at all.
As to cultivating the friendfhip of my
hufband, we are very civil when we meet,
but we are both too much engaged to fpend
much time with each other. With regard
to my daughters, I have given them a
French governefs, and proper mafters, I
can do no more for them. You tell me
I fhould inftruct my fervants, but I have
no time to inform myfelf, much lefs can

I undertake any thing of that fort for
them, or even be able to guefs what they
do with themfelves the greater part of the
twenty-four hours. I go to church, if
poffible, once on a Sunday, and then fome
of my fervants attend me; and if they
will not mind what the preacher fays, how
can I help it? The management of our
fortune, as far as I am concerned, I muft
leave to the fteward and houfekeeper; for
I find I can barely fnatch a quarter of an
hour juft to look over the bill of fare when
I am to have company, that they may not
fend up any thing frightful or old-fafhion-
ed. As to the Chriftian duty of charity, I
affure you I am not ill-natured; and (confidering that the great expenfe of being
always dreft for company, with loffes at
cards, fubfcriptions, and public fpectacles,
leave me very little to difpofe of,) I am
ready enough to give my money when I
meet with a miferable object. You fay
I fhould inquire out fuch, inform myfelf
thoroughly of their cafes, make an acquaintance with the poor in my neighbourhood in the country, and plan out
the beft methods of relieving the unfortu-
nate, and affifting the induftrious, but this

fuppofes much more time, and much more
money, than I have to beſtow. I have had
hopes, indeed, that my ſummers would
have afforded me more leiſure, but we ſtay
pretty late in town, then we generally
paſs ſeveral weeks at one or other of the
water-drinking places, where every moment is ſpent in public; and, for the few
months in which we reſide at our own
ſeat, our houſe is always full with a ſuc-
ceſſion of company, to whoſe amuſement
one is obliged to dedicate every hour of
the day."

THE READING CONTINUED.

I have here given you a ſpecimen of a
life ſpent in unprofitable toil and unſatiſ-
fying pleaſures. No pleaſures are ſatiſfy-
ing, or worthy of a rational being, but
ſuch as are conſiſtent with religion and
virtue. I will here give you, from the
ſame author, an account of a family whoſe
manner of living differs conſiderably from
that of the lady you have juſt been reading about.

"Sir Charles and Lady Worthy are
neither gloomy aſcetics, nor frantic en-

H

thufiafts; they married from affection, on
long acquaintance and perfect efteem;
they therefore enjoy the beft pleafures of
the heart in the higheft degree. They
concur in a rational fcheme of life, which,
whilft it makes them always cheerful and
happy, renders them the friends of human kind, and the blefling of all around
them. They do not defert their ftation
in the world, nor deny themfelves the
proper and moderate ufe of their large fortune; though that portion of it which is
appropriated to the ufe of others, is that
from which they derive their higheft gratifications. They fpend four or five months
every year in London, where they keep
up an intercourfe of hofpitality and civility
with many of the moft refpectable perfons
of their own or of higher rank: but they
have endeavoured rather at a *felect* than a
numerous acquaintance; and as they never play cards, this endeavour has the
more eafily fucceeded. Three days in the
week, from the hour of dinner, are given
up to this intercourfe with what may be
called the world. Three more are fpent
in a family way, with a few intimate
friends, whofe taftes are conformable to

their own, and with whom the book and working-table, or sometimes music, supply the intervals of useful and agreeable conversation. In these parties their children are always present, and partake of the improvement that arises from the well-chosen pieces which are read aloud. The seventh day is always spent at home, after the due attendance on public worship ; and it is peculiarly appropriated to the religious instruction of their children and servants, or to other works of charity. As they keep regular hours, and rise early, and as Lady Worthy never pays or admits morning visits, they have seven or eight hours in every day free from all interruptions from the world, in which the cultivation of their own minds, and those of their children, the due attention to health, to economy, and to the poor, are carried on in the most regular manner.

"Thus, even in London, they contrive, without the appearance of quarrelling with the world, or of shutting themselves up from it, to pass the greater part of their time in a reasonable and useful, as well as an agreeable manner. The rest of the

H 2

year they spend at their family-seat in the
country, where the happy effects of their
example, and of their assiduous attention
to the good of all around them, are still
more observable than in town. Their
neighbours, their tenants, and the poor for
many miles about them, find in them a
sure resource and comfort in calamity, and
a ready assistance in every scheme of ho-
nest industry. The young are instructed
at their expense, and under their direc-
tion, and rendered useful at the earliest
period possible; the aged and the sick
have every comfort administered that their
state requires; the idle and dissolute are
kept in awe by vigilant inspection; the
quarrelsome are brought, by a sense of
their own interest, to live more quietly
with their family and neighbours, and
amicably to refer their disputes to Sir
Charles's decision.

"This amiable pair are not less highly
prized by the genteel families of their
neighbourhood, who are sure of finding in
their house the most polite and cheerful
hospitality, and in them a fund of good
sense and good humour, with a constant
disposition to promote every innocent plea-

sure. They are particularly the delight of all the young people, who consider them as their patrons and their oracles, to whom they always apply for advice and assistance in any kind of distress, or in any scheme of amusement.

"Sir Charles and Lady Worthy are seldom without some friends in the house with them during their stay in the country; but, as their methods are known, they are never broken in upon by their guests, who do not expect to see them till dinner-time, except at the hour of prayer, and at breakfast. In their private walks or rides, they usually visit the cottages of the labouring poor, with all of whom they are personally acquainted; and by the sweetness and friendliness of their manner, as well as by their beneficent actions they so entirely possess the hearts of these people, that they are made confidants of all their family grievances, and the casuists to settle all their scruples of conscience or difficulties in conduct. By this method of conversing freely with them, they find out their different characters and capacities, and often discover and apply to their own benefit, as well as that of the perſon they diſtinguiſh, talents which would otherwiſe have been for ever loſt to the public."

What a charming deſcription of well-regulated life do we find here! What tranquillity, what true enjoyment in the "beſt pleaſures of friendſhip, of parental and family affeċtion, of divine beneficence, and a piety which chiefly conſiſts in joyful aċts of love and praiſe!"

ELDEST BOY.

We muſt remember, my young friends, that to-morrow is the Sabbath-day; let us retire early, that we may riſe betimes, and attend to the duties of that holy day.

Early in the morning we meet, if Heaven ſo will, and prepare our minds for public worſhip; and when the night comes, if our uſual Sunday evening's avocations allow us time, we will go forward with our little book, as I ſee it concludes with the ſubjeċt of

RELIGION.

THE SEVENTH EVENING.

ELDEST BOY.

"Come learn the way;
"Wouldst thou have a pleasant evening,
"Spend well the day."

I hope this, and every evening of our lives, will enable us to bear testimony to the truth of this axiom.

―――――――

THE SEVENTH EVENING's READING.

My young friends, the seventh portion of reading is intended, if time and occasions permit, for a Sunday's evening. We must, therefore, confine ourselves to subjects suitable to the evening of that day which we are commanded, from the highest authority, *to keep holy.*

The subjects I fix on, then, for this night's reading are these: The duty of public worship—The efficacy of prayer—And the necessity of forming religious principles at an early age.

PUBLIC WORSHIP OF GOD.

"It is evident both from reafon and fcripture, that public worfhip is a moft ufeful and indifpenfable duty. It is equally evident, that if this duty *is* to be performed, fome fixed and ftated *time* for the performing it is abfolutely neceffary; for without this, it is impoffible that any number of perfons can ever be collected together in one place. Now one day in feven feems to be as proper and convenient a portion of our time to be allotted to this ufe, as any other that can be named. The returns of it are frequent enough to keep alive the fenfe of religion in our hearts, and diftant enough to leave a very fufficient interval for our worldly concerns.

If then this time was fixed only by the laws, or even by the cuftoms of our country, it would be our duty and our wifdom to comply with it. Confidering it merely as *an ancient ufage*, yet, if antiquity can render an ufage venerable, this muft be of all others the *moft* venerable, for it is coeval with the world itfelf. But it had, moreover, the fanction of a divine command, From the very beginning of time, God bleffed and fanctified the feventh day to the purpofes of religion *. That injunction was again repeated to the Jews, in the moft folemn manner, at the promulgation of their law from Mount Sinai †, and once more urged upon them by Mofes, " Keep the Sabbath-day, to fanctify it, as the Lord thy God hath commanded thee ‡."

After our Lord's refurrection, the *firft* day of the week was, in memory of that great event, fubftituted in the room of the *feventh* ; and from that time to the prefent, that is, for almoft eighteen hundred years, it has been conftantly fet apart for the public worfhip of God by the whole Chrift-ian world ; and, whatever difference of opinion there may have been in other re-fpects, in this all parties, fects, and deno-minations of Chriftians have univerfally

* Gen. ii. 3.　　　† Exod. xx. 8, 9, 10, 11. ‡ Deut. v. 12.

and invariably agreed By thefe means it comes to pafs, that on this day many *millions of people*, are at one and the fame time engaged in profirating themfelves before the throne of Grace, and offering up their facrifice of prayer, praife, and thankfgiving to the common Lord of all, " in whom they live, and move, and have their being."

There is in this view of the Lord's day fomething fo wonderfully awful and magnificent, that one would think it almoft impoffible for any man to refift the inclination he muft find in himfelf to join in this general affembly of the human race ; " to go with the multitude," as the Pfalmift expreffes it, " into the houfe of God," and to take a part in a folemnity fo ftriking to the imagination, fo fuitable to the Majefty of Heaven, fo adapted to the wants, the neceffities, the infirmities, the obligations, and the duties of a created and a dependent being !

The importance of a ferious and devout obfervance of the Lord's day is moft emphatically recommended, in a difcourfe on

that fubject, by the prefent bifhop of London, from whence the above is taken *.

SONG

On the Public Obfervance of the LORD's DAY.

I.

How glorious 'tis to fee the throng
   Beneath yon vaulted roof attend ;
Whence pious pray'r, and humble fong,
   On wings of Faith and Hope afcend !

II.

Who would not quit each bufy care?
   Who would not each vain pleafure fhun?
Who but with joy would haften there,
   And join the praifes thus begun ?

III.

How doth th' enraptur'd heart expand,
   To think that in this blifsful hour,
Re-echo'd from each diftant land,
   An UNIVERSAL PRAYER we pour.

---

* Sermons on feveral Subjects, by the Rev.
Beilby Porteous, D. D. then Bifhop of Chefter,
(now Bifhop of London,) publifhed 1783.

IV.

This *hour*, then, let us all repair
  To celebrate our Maker's praife;
O ! let our voices fill the air,
  And join th' Archangels' choral lays!

F. A.

Since the obfervance of the Sabbath is
founded upon fo many wife and juft reafons, what have they to anfwer for, who
not only negleæ this inftitution themfelves,
but bring it by their example into contempt with others? I fpeak not to thofe
who make it a day of common diverfion;
who, laying afide all decency, and break-
ing through all civil and religious regula-
tions, fpend it in the moft licentious
amufements: Such people are paft all re-
proof; but I fpeak to thofe who, in other
things, profefs to be ferious people, and
who, one would hope, would aæ right,
when they were convinced what was fo*.

Having fpoken of public worfhip, let
us now fay a few words on the ufe and
efficacy of *prayer in general.*

---

* GILPIN.

There is one motive to this duty, far more conftraining than all others that can be named, more imperious than any argument on its utility, than any convictions of its efficacy, even any experience of its confolations. *Prayer is the command of God;* the plain, pofitive, repeated injunction of the Moft High, who declares, " He will be inquired of." This is enough to fecure the obedience of a Chriftian, even though a promife were not, as it always is, attached to the command. But in this cafe, to our unfpeakable comfort, the promife is as clear as the precept, " *Afk*, and ye fhall *receive; feek*, and ye fhall *find;* knock, and it fhall be opened to you." This is encouragement enough for the plain Chriftian. It is enough for him, that *thus faith the Lord.* When a ferious Chriftian has once got a plain unequivocal command from his Maker on any point, he never fufpends his obedience, while he is amufing himfelf with looking about for fubordinate motives of action. Inftead of curioufly analyzing the nature of the duty, he confiders how he fhall beft fulfil it *.

---

* HANNAH MORE.

I

As it is the effect of prayer to *expand* the affections, as well as to *sanctify* them, the benevolent Christian is not satisfied to commend himself alone to the divine favour. The heart which is full of the love of God, will overflow with love to its neighbour. All that are near to himself, he wishes to bring near to God.

———

Necessity of gaining Habits of Attention and Virtue, and of forming Religious Principles at an early Age.

The great use of knowledge in all its various branches, is to free the mind from the prejudices of ignorance, and to give it juster and more enlarged conceptions, than are the mere growth of rude nature. By reading, you add the experience of others to your own. It is the improvement of the mind chiefly, that makes the difference between man and man; and gives one man a real superiority over another.

Befides, the mind muft be employed.
The lower orders of men have their attention much engroffed by thofe employments, in which the neceffities of
life engage them; and it is happy that
they have. Labour ftands in the room of
education, and fills up thofe vacancies of
mind which, in a ftate of idlenefs, would
be engroffed by vice. And if they, who
have more leifure, do not fubftitute fomething in the room of this, their minds alfo
will become the prey of vice; and the
more fo, as they have the means to indulge it more in their power. If then
the mind muft be employed, what can
fill up its vacancies more rationally than
the acquifition of knowledge? Let us
therefore thank God for the opportunities
he hath afforded us; and not turn into a
curfe thofe means of leifure, which might
become fo great a bleffing. But however
neceffary knowledge may be, religion,
we know, is infinitely more fo. The one
adorns a man, and gives him, it is true,
fuperiority and rank in life; but the other
is abfolutely effential to his happinefs.

I 2

In the midst of youth, health, and abundance, the world is apt to appear a very gay and pleasing scene; it engages our desires; and, in a degree, satisfies them also. But it is wisdom to consider, that a time will come when youth, health, and fortune will fail us; and if disappointment and vexation do not sour our taste for pleasure, at least sickness and infirmities will destroy it. In these gloomy seasons and above all at the approach of death, what will become of us without religion? When this world fails us, where shall we fly, if we expect no refuge in another?

For improvement in knowledge, youth is certainly the fittest season. The mind is then ready to receive any impression. It is free from all that care and attention which, in riper age, the affairs of life bring with them. The memory too is then stronger and better able to acquire the rudiments of knowledge; besides, there is sometimes in youth a modesty and ductility, which in advanced years, if those years especially have been left a prey to ignorance, become self-sufficiency and prejudice; and these effectually bar up all the inlets to knowledge. But, above all, unlefs habits of attention and application are early gained, we fhall fcarce acquire them afterwards. The inconfiderate youth feldom reflects upon this; nor knows his lofs, till he knows alfo that it cannot be retrieved.

Nor is youth more the feafon to acquire knowledge, than to form religious habits. It is a great point to get *habit* on the fide of *virtue*. It will make every thing fmooth and eafy. The earlieft principles are generally the moft lafting; and thofe of a religious caft are feldom wholly loft. Though the temptations of the world may, now and then, draw the well-principled youth afide, yet his principles being continually at war with his practice, there is hope, that in the end the better part may overcome the worfe, and bring on a reformation. Whereas, he who has fuffered habits of vice to get poffeffion of his youth, has little chance of being brought back to a fenfe of religion. In a common courfe of things, it can rarely happen. Some calamity muft roufe him. He muft be awakened by a ftorm, or fleep for ever."

I 3

Piety to God is the foundation of good morals; and is a difpofition particularly graceful and becoming to youth. To be void of it, argues a cold heart—defitute of fome of the beft affections which belong to that age. Youth is the feafon of warm and generous emotions. The heart fhould then fpontaneoufly rife into the admiration of what is great; glow with the love of what is fair and excellent; and melt at the difcovery of tendernefs and goodnefs. Where can an object be found fo proper to kindle thofe affections as the Father of the univerfe, and the Author of all felicity? Unmoved by veneration, can you contemplate that grandeur and majefty which his works every where difplay? Untouched by gratitude, can you view that profufion of good, which, in this pleafing feafon of life, his beneficent hand pours around you? Happy in the love and affection of thofe with whom you are connected, look up to the Supreme Being, as the infpirer of all the friendfhip which has ever been fhown you by others; himfelf your beft, and your firft friend; formerly the fupporter of your infancy, and the guide of your childhood, now the guardian of your youth, and the hope of your coming years.

Do not imagine, that when exhorted to be religious, you are called upon to become more formal and folemn in your manners than others of the fame years; or to erect yourfelves into fupercilious reprovers of thofe around you. The fpirit of true religion breathes gentlenefs and affability. It gives a native unaffected eafe to the behaviour. It is focial, kind, and cheerful; far removed from that gloomy and illiberal fuperftition which clouds the brow, fharpens the temper, dejects the fpirits, and teaches men to fit themfelves for another world, by neglecting the concerns of this. Let your religion, on the contrary, connect preparation for heaven with an honourable difcharge of the duties of active life. Of fuch religion difcover, on every proper occafion, that you are not afhamed * !

* BLAIR.

ELDEST BOY.

I, for one, am not aſhamed of ſuch religion, but glory in it.—So do we all.

Youth certainly is the ſeaſon to acquire
knowledge, and to form religious habits.
Let us keep this in our minds; by endeavouring to do ſo, we ſhall not be the leſs
cheerful. This little book has ſufficiently
proved to us, that to be good is to be
happy. " There is no peace, ſaith the
Lord, for the wicked."

_____

We have now completed the Seven
Evenings' Readings. The laſt will, I truſt,
have repreſented religion to you in ſo
amiable a light, that you will walk cheer-
fully in her pleaſant ways to the end of a
happy life. " Her ways are ways of
pleaſantneſs, and all her paths are peace:"
but this is not all; they lead to glory, to
everlaſting joy.—Now, having ſpent well
the day, the Lord's Day I mean, let me
intreat you to " bring the ſpirit of the
Sunday's devotion into the tranſactions of
the week," and let it influence your future lives.

I cannot clofe this little book without expreffing my earneft and beft wifhes for the welfare of this fociety, and of all the little focieties for whofe ufe it is intended. You have my earneft prayers for your improvement in grace and ufeful knowledge, for your temporal and eternal happinefs; and if the great Difpofer of all events fhall permit me to be, in fome degree, inftrumental to your attainment of thefe bleffings, though it fhould be only in a fingle inftance, I fhall ever look back with delight on the hours fo devoted to your fervice.

A Friend of Youth.

By WILSON and SPENCE, York,

THE ENGLISH READER:

Or, PIECES IN PROSE AND POETRY, felected from the BEST WRITERS. Defigned to affift young Perfons to read with Propriety and Effect; to improve their Language and Sentiments; and to inculcate fome of the moft important Principles of Piety and Virtue. With a few preliminary Obfervations on the Principles of Good Reading.

By LINDLEY MURRAY,

Author of "Englifh Grammar adapted to the different Claffes of Learners," &c. The Third Edition. Price, bound, 4s.

Where may be had, by the fame Author,

1. ENGLISH GRAMMAR, adapted to the different Claffes of Learners. With an Appendix, containing Rules and Obfervations, for affifting the more advanced Students to write with Perfpicuity and Accuracy, 7th edition, corrected and improved. Price, bound, 3s. 6d.

2. An ABRIDGMENT of L. MUR-RAY's ENGLISH GRAMMAR. With an Appendix, containing an Exemplification of the Parts of Speech. Defigned for the younger Clafs of Learners. Price, bound, 1s.

3. ENGLISH EXERCISES, adapted to the Grammar lately publifhed by L. MUR-RAY; confifting of Exemplifications of the Parts of Speech; Inftances of Falfe Orthography; Violations of the Rules of Syntax; Defects in Punctuation; and Violations of the Rules refpecting Perfpicuity and Accuracy. Defigned for the Benefit of Private Learners, as well as for the Ufe of Schools. Price, bound, 2s. 6d.

4. A KEY to the Englifh Exercifes; calculated to enable private Learners, to become their own Inftructors in Grammar and Compofition. Price, bound, 2s.
The Exercifes and the Key may be had together. Price, bound, 4s.

5. THE POWER OF RELIGION ON THE MIND, in Retirement, Affliction, and at the Approach of Death; Exempli-

Lightning Source UK Ltd.
Milton Keynes UK
UKHW020736210621
385893UK00007B/831